Daydreams & Deep Dimples: Beneath the smile

Amira Sims

BookLeaf Publishing

India | USA | UK

Presentation by *BookLeaf Publishing*

Web: www.bookleafpub.com

E-mail: info@bookleafpub.com

ISBN: 978-93-5744-343-2

First edition 2022

DEDICATION

To all those who exist where the words on a
page are enough to soothe the pain in your heart
and the ugly in the world.

ACKNOWLEDGEMENT

Author's photo and make-up by K.L Bray 2016.

Rethinking Old Sayings

I have heard the statement that a hard head
makes a soft behind, but what I now know to be
true is that the soft behind is not from being
spanked by mom or pop

Hard times make you realize some real truths

Truth#1 you have to endure some discomfort if
you want to have a certain level of satisfaction

I'm committed to a more pleasing smile and so
I've endured gum surgery 3 times, dental tourism
by way of 8 Costa Rican porcelain veneers, and
now braces, countless professional cleanings, an
unspeakable amount of brushing my teeth,
flossing, gargling with Listerine

The effort to keep my palate clean has been real,
consistent, and effortful

In much the same way I am committed to being
financially free

Independence can be purchased

12 years a slave taught me that Jim Rohn was
right

it's not about how much per hour, it's about skills
and the value you bring to the marketplace

Bring value and you get perks

Convert those perks and like George Classon
and Richard Kiyosaki said your money will
work for you

That's the secret

HARNESS your best YOU

Nurture that unique/ iris of a brain

FIND your peace and your purpose and you will
find

your paradise

Sounds that Birth Clarity

When you really hear the lion roar
it obliterates your soul
and you understand the soul of my people

When you feel the warmth of the sun
the rays heat up an inner universe of cells
and you can smile through the pain

When you smell the rain
the odor can be pleasant because it
reminds you that the earth is home for now

All the insight I need to know I can gather from
the combination of my senses

SAMO/ DEI

A sea of peach is what I see when I look out into
the crowd
It's what she saw when she was on stage

We glide around smoothly in worlds of isolation,
separated by 36 years

Nevertheless, we are both

Interacting, engaging, absorbing, emitting
And realizing

Our difference

In talks of diversity, equity, and inclusion there
are so many conversations that are silenced

Or are they the silent songs of the diverse that
are whispers, meant only to be spoken in hushed
tones

For fear that they would loudly crush the
narrative that DEI programs want to overlook

If your intent is to jazz up dinner with new
spices and new dishes then let's start by adding
some additional sue chefs and realizing that we
can't maintain the same paradigm and expect
different results

Yes some new recipes are in order but if the
same chefs are preparing them, dare I say there
will be something similar to a regression toward
the average

How did Basquait phrase it, SAMO

We can't have a figurehead that is representative
of the need to be more inclusive

But then in our actual pursuits, we serve the
same dishes, simply rearranged on the plate

More salt, less pepper but no cayenne pepper

More salt, perhaps we will try some pink sea salt

But

Turmeric has a different texture and flavor

I am constantly inspired to aspire for a truth that
I am uncertain if I will ever realize

My beloved APA and even APA's IPI still falls
short despite good intentions

The work is solid

The inspiration was true

Those involved were sincere

But

What I don't want is more of the same

I am Organized Chaos

I am a living contradiction.
Intellect and fashion simultaneously hold my attention.
I'm thriving due to the duality of my African and American roots.
My shoe game and book game are in competition. My passion for art is rivaled by my admiration for science.
I adore man-made and natural things.
I'm living my best life and simultaneously striving to make the world a better place.
I have come to realize that my desire to teach stems from my yearning for learning.
Life is less about dichotomies and more about discovery.
At this stage in life, I'm embracing the organized chaos that is mi.

Enter Into Darkness

I'm trying to be optimistic, I've sunk my roots in
the soil
I've volunteered my time
My energy
Invested sweat
Blood
Bile
I've given of myself and what is my reward
More work
More toil
And I give thanks for that

Right now, I feel desperate
I feel like fuck it
Like I'm tired of trying
I'm tired of the cycle
I get why people kill themselves
It's so sexy
The door
The portal to a new unknown space that might
be a relief from the pain of
Racism
And childbirth
The pain of unwanted mental pregnancies

Unwanted abortions of dreams
Undesired tainting of my once pristine soul
The choking
The spitting on
The slapping in the face
The abandonment of freedom
The task of toiling for someone else
The task of being a surrogate
And meanwhile
They don't get it
They don't know

But ill keep singing the tunes
5 5 w brown eyes—anything I want I got it

I need drugs
I want to be numb
It hurts
So bad
I want to cut myself and just let the blood flow
from my veins and lay on a dirty floor and
escape from this terrible life that is called
happily ever after
No one gets it
They say they do but they don't

I'm so sick of being strong
And sick of being weak
I'll be in the class A team

I got to go into the recesses of my mind for any
solace
Any peace
The only voice that comforts me is mine

So fuck off
Tune me out
I don't want to hear it will get better
I don't want to hear about the silver lining
I just want to wallow in this emotion because
this sadness and pain is just as much a reality as
the joy that comes in the morning
The happiness of that news
That I got the job
That I got the feature
That my dad and mom loves me and that the
crush thinks im cute too
But right now
All those pleasant fragrances
Escape my nostrils
All the wonderful tunes don't allow vibrations
And I have entered into darkness
I am embracing the pain
I will bear down and understand that I must be
dilated to 10 centimeters
What will I push out
What will come out of this?
When I emerge from darkness what will come
with me

What cries of joy will echo in whose chambers?

Depression

Depression sounds like a sleepless night that just
never ends and your'e still not rested
It sounds like "I need a drink"
It sounds like "I don't want to get up",
"life sucks"

Depression is a love song that is on repeat in the
background because the lyrics are so painful but
true that you don't care that you haven't
showered, you can't remember the last time you
smelled the roses- what's the point in planning
for the future

Depression hurts
It kills
It is real

It's a movie reel that keeps telling you to press
pause on the things you once enjoyed or better
yet turn off the channel that be your pathetic life

Depression smells like the meals you skip
It smells like bad breath
Like you know, the breath that doesn't deserve
to be taken

Depression hurts
It kills
It steals
It is real

April Blues

4.8.21
I'm learning to curb my ambition and to cry
I'm centering myself and trying the way of the
way
Where there is no good
No bad
Just existence

4.9.21
We did the dance. I slicked my hair back as best
I could for someone with natural locs who has
no care of tightening and taming god's roots. I
put on lipstick to accentuate the fullness of what
would come from my mouth.
I reviewed their website. I showed up on time. I
prepared a lesson and I learned that the dance is
for me. No, they haven't called. No, they
probably won't call but that's fine.

Know thyself. Know thy worth.

I am but a ship sailing for distant lands. I meet
turbulent waters and gusty winds. The sun bakes
my deck and I'm comforted by the calmness that
keeps me afloat.

I am the sun that shines hard and lasts long. I am
the moon that controls gravitational pools and
women's bleeding.
I am the grass that cows eat.
I am me
And I'm ok.

No, they won't call with good news, so stop
hoping. I tell myself. I talk to myself in my own
form of poetry and find beauty in it. I am
disgusted by the world but the world is also a
part of me so I continue to inhale and exhale.
The cycles of war, peace, war, peace, hatred,
strife, love, grief and ecstasy continue as far as I
can see.

Sail away hope. Sail away misfortune. Sail away
but don't stray from the goal. I am a teacher. I
push falsehoods aside. I accept the weight of the
crown. My royal lineage couldn't be tainted
despite man's depravity. I will sparkle anyway
because
I am me
And I'm ok.

Colorless

I know why you say you don't see color
I don't see my ever expanding waistline

I want to bury my head in the sand too

Ignorance feels bliss but it causes blisters

We have to do the uncomfortable
If we want change

We have to push past this stage
Rage is the appropriate response
When you get as angry about racism as you are
about bad customer service and someone
infringing on your personal rights
Then we can have a real conversation
When you get as ashamed of the real history of
this country –this legacy of abuse, misuse, and
miseducation—as you are of Trumps actions
Then we can have a real conversation

Until then stfu
Until then be silent
Until then pause

Meditate
Talk to the hand because I will not be your yes
ma'am

When you are ready—ill be ready
We can stroll down repair street together
We can sip reparations tea and recite the
repatriation treaty
We can sing and dance and teach our great grans
about revolutions and we can be merry together
We can honor martyrs together and talk about
that time when you thought we were stupid
enough to believe that putting Biden in the white
house was going to whitewash his racist past

We can color in one of the intricate adult
coloring books together and revive a piece of the
American pineapple that was buried under the
sea

I sometimes imagine the tea party those Africans
who jumped had as they refused to let you use
their bodies
I sometimes hear my ancestors whisper in my
ear and visit me in my dreams and remind me to
remember my greatness
To remember that they were triumphant that
Sankofa is real

That the Japanese principle of Wabi-Sabi is an
African proverb

I am ancient wisdom turned modern-day dummy
I am recovering parts of me that have been
buried in those seas
I am unearthing an inner strength that withstood
what no other manner of flesh could
And so I do see the colors of the rainbow and I
see you wishing and longing and hoping for
salvation from that ship
But salvation is being salvaged by the savages
Salvation sees color.
Salvation is appreciating that all humans bleed
red
That the blue sky shines on us all
That brown is not an ugly color it produces life
and sustains us all
That green can be the color of greed or
something completely different
Yellow is a mocking bird that wasn't killed or
mocked or shunned it is the color of the sun
And black- well black absorbs all colors.

Writing Endless Possibilities

Somewhere between reading emails, watching TikTok reels, chauffeuring my kids, washing dishes, and dealing with the bullshit of being a black woman in a white man's world, I find time to be me. I carve out a little space to write, to draw, to breath, to exist. In these spaces, although time is limited, my focus and my belief in the ability to make things better are limitless.

10.6.2020

Inspired by an image of a statue being pulled
down with roots still intact

my thoughts...yes let's pull down the statues but
if you want to stop there, then miss me

miss me with your inauthentic I don't see color
while waiving your rainbow flag and saying blue
lives matter self

miss me with your I love everyone meanwhile
you have no problem with talking about visitors
to this country as illegal aliens--since when did
alienation become legal--oh that's right I forgot

we are in the united snakes of Amerikkka

don't let the anger fool you

don't panic and freak out cause I'm holding a
fake sword during cosplay

don't shoot me cause you got a toy gun that
killed me 9 times over while I prayed for this
land

while I committed myself to ending ww2 you
saw no need to salute my valor

honor me in your sleep as I sleep on the discord
you have sowed across the globe

but Cain slew able

and his brothers sold Joseph into slavery

and Bathsheba lover sent her husband into war

and I'm up because spirits be talking to me

they tell me to pick up my pen and write

they whisper in my ears and make my mind keep
spinning and delighting in nonsense that is not
perceived by those without this 6th sense

all the while I am accepting my love of this
place

the people who I love are here

I was born here

It's hard to escape, to run to freedom

When I get a taste of freedom with every student
I reach

I smell freedom when I see the flowers in my
garden being tended to by the butterflies

I hear freedom with every crazy dance move I
make

Freedom rings as Oprah becomes Amerikkas
matriarch

Freedom is reborn on every mlkjr street when
gunshots become the norm

A free world exists here in these united snakes
of Amerikkka

And I'm missing my mentors

I'm hearing Marcus Mariah and I ain't talking
about Mariah Carey

I'm hearing Nina and yes it is Simone

I'm hearing Ertha

I feel so connected to people I cant see

Cause I see dead people with my mind's eye

I have senestatia – im a sensaste

A tortured soul who decided to roll with the
punches

Bring it on spirit

I'll write your words

You can use my voice

You can use my tongue

You can use my hands

I'm here for it

I don't taste dirt yet

Another Pill to Swallow

I feel so hollow inside because it's like no one
understands my plight
the words I write
they don't bring life to the emotions that are
bottled up inside
if I speak, I'm heard
but when I try to speak
my words escape me and my voice can't bring
forth the fruits of my thoughts
am I lost?

When I left the house the other day my man said
to me
beat them off with a bat
and I was like
yeah right
I can't see why he thinks I'm a walking beauty
because
I'm so concerned about the state of my inner
beauty
I have a hard time demanding respect
because I lack the desire to be overly aggressive
but that's my problem, the words that are in my
heart they are full of power
they need a voice to give them their due

but when I try to speak
my words escape me and my voice can bring
forth the fruits of my thoughts

A long time ago I worked with an old man that
had 75 years under his belt
He swallowed 14 pills daily, this is true
but those pills aint nothing like the pills I have to
swallow

See, society tells me to open my mouth and open
wide
but I say
open up your minds

you and I
we are a part of the generation that is asked to
accept the possible reality of the discovery of the
missing link between man and ape

you and I
we are a part of the generation that is asked to
associate the word breast with sex and not with
baby

we are supposed to teach our children about
Santa clause and the tooth fairy in one breath
and tell them not to lie in the next

you and I
we are part of the generation that is asked to
believe that 911 was the greatest tragedy of all
times
like this was the first time innocent lives were
lost

but what about the mass genocide that has
systematically destroyed a population of people

what about the millions of brown-eyed boys and
girls at the bottom of some ocean somewhere

it's not that I'm arrogant
and it's not that I'm shy

I see the world through a different set of eyes
and
sometimes
I feel like it's me and then there's everyone else

but I know that its people out there that feel me

when you are a woman
your worth, your value as a person isn't
determined by how sexy you are

and its not about talking about being strong
strength lies in actions

speaking lipservice to quench my appetite for
recognition doesn't make me strong

no
my strength comes from supporting my man
my strength comes from raising my boys to be
real men
my strength comes from not being intimidated
by being one of the only African Americans in
my program of study at the time

my strength is expressed in my unwillingness to
bow down to the conditions of worth the
American society places on me

I don't have to be first
I don't have to be last
My hair don't have to be straight
and
My nails don't need to be painted
I can think for myself and speak for myself
I can choose to swallow the pills placed before
me or I can choose to push them aside
I can accept the responsibility of earning respect
and I can strive to be beautiful inside and out
I can be
Amira
Hanifah
Sims

I can be me
and that's ok

Confession

Confession
I like my poetry
I like my spoken words
No one can tell me anything
I'm an artist and I'm sensitive about my "shit"
Cause it aint shit, it's a series of masterful
expressions

Its alchemy
It's me taking the pain of this world and
converting it into something palatable
It's me wearing my armor and simultaneously
making music with my design choices
It's me singing with my strides
It's me sighing with my snides

Breath

With no breath, we sing from our bellies
We play wind instruments
We create wind storms

With no air
Not being able to breath
And
We breathe through our skin
We breathe through our hair
We breathe through our hips

Our legs create gills
Our dance generates gusts of air
Don't tell me I aint magic

You better get out of here with that (SHIT)
The precision of our breaths rejuvenates our
ancestors' culture
A hidden language comes out in clarinet
playing, flutists flaunting their implicit
knowledge
Our audacity to exist, to survive, to overcome
…to cry out from the ground -from the ocean
Like the phoenix….like Sankofa…

We breathe
We live
We excite this world with our ability to breath
Despite their attempts to crush our windpipes
To silence our splendor
To make our candor mute

We make mutations of this thing called breath
That dash between born and died is all about the
breath
He couldn't breathe and now the world knows of
his life

I remember breathing through the contractions
Breathing through the excitement
Breathing as I sighed and accepted that news

Living is breathing
Breath is life

Writing

When I feel like this I write
It's all I can do
Sometimes the words dance on the page and
mingle in a pleasing way and others call it
poetry
I call it a diary entry
I call it relief
The shit of this world gets so smelly that I have
to open the windows and doors
I have to allow the toxicity to escape the
crevices of my mind least I take the path of
Bourdain or Robin Williams

Life is no joke and then it is simultaneously the
funniest pain that ever there was
Here I lay
Fingers sore from manual labor
Heart heavy with hope and hopelessness

Eyes raw from tears that finally escaped
Toe throbbing
Teeth tired of being caged in bob wire
Throat longing for words with friends
Vajayjay neglected

Blah
Disgust is a genuine emotion
And so ill write
I'll write to keep my sanity and ill write because
it is insanity not to
I'll write because ever since I was a little kid I
learned that writing is my secret hiding place
I can escape to this other place where miraisms
are acceptable
Where I am me and everything is ok

A Suicide Love Song

Life sucks. They don't tell you that for every
half of a good time there will be hell on earth to
pay. For the excitement and hope of a new love a
fresh start there are a thousand deaths. For an
investment of time, money, energy what do you
get—tears, papercuts, pain, devastation,
nightmares a hurt that is only masked by drugs
and alcohol. Being American was never easy.
Being black was never wrong nor right it just is.
There is no healing when the assault is
everlasting.
These kids are not giving me joy.
These degrees ain't giving me security.
There is no solace in my so-called good looks.
Health is an illusion.

I hate life.
I really do. I'm too stubborn to kill myself but I
don't like this.
I've tried too hard for too long with no results.

I have nothing to say to anyone.

Every disappointment breeds resentment and
contentment.

Every breath erases memories of good times
while solidifying the engraved marks of the
trauma of being born in this place, to this race,
in this time, without a dime
It's criminal for me to believe in happy days and
a brighter future
It's worthless to dream of peace when war is the
language of these streets
I am hopeless
I am here
And I'm so tired of showing up
So tired of trying
So tired of giving it my best fucking effort

And that's when I was introduced to Zen
To clear a cluttered mind
Delete your concept of mind

To stop the tears from falling
Recognize that every dry earth needs rain

To stop the stomach from churning
Remember the contractions and the ring of fire
and the new births

Remember New Birth (missionary Baptist
church)
Remember – re-member
Sankofa is my salvation

Sankofa is my satisfaction
Sankofa is my savior
I'll savor Sankofa

And

Peace rushes in like a gentle breeze just when
you need it the most

There must be a silver lining
I'm here for it

Don't tell me it will get better
Tell me the truth—it will get worst
The only date I have is with a dirt nap
The only thing sacred is understanding that you
are worthless

Maybe that's what's meant by let go and let god
Succumb to the fantasy
Enjoy the delusion
Embrace the fuckery

Friends are the only thing life is worth living for
And even they can't fully get you
And do you want to burden them

Dan Eades, I get you

Moody

If words had no meaning would you understand
me? Somehow the rhythm in my breath is the
blues in your heart
If time stood still and the rain never stopped
pouring down from the heavens
Would you sit with me and listen to the frogs
delight in this harmonious interaction
This exchange of notes
This melody of life

All the world is a beautiful love song with its
melancholic highs and lows
A stage to perform a poem
A dance to be done alone and with a partner and
in a line

What are we?
A species … a flesh… a people… a collection of
misconceptions
A dare to be all that we wish we were

And then I am reminded that I am here
In this place…not quite sunken but sinking

Shying away from embracing the sounds of
youth
Ignoring the cries of bloody murder from the
ground
Standing still in the face of that jazzy melody
that makes you want to move your body

Oh body, oh to be able to transcend time

I sat with myself

I sat with myself, knee to chest contemplating
how I have been treated since I relocated to the
South
Cast aside. Used to check a diversity box, to
ease the shame of being not racist but not having
any friends with melanin

Neglecting my peace to grab a piece of the
American pie –the lie that I am a second-class
citizen, a hyphenated American

I poured out my feelings of disconnection and
disillusionment in my poems
When there is nothing left
I honor my ancestors
I pay homage to their struggle and their progress

I feel their breath on my neck sometimes
I receive kindness from strangers who are Black,
White, Asian, other
And I remember that humanity can't be carved
into boxes to check
We are all connected—we strive together—we
rise together

There are times when being still is priceless
Knowing that post-traumatic growth is a thing
And
When my mind is quieted, there are soulful
moments that renew my willingness to believe in
that thing called hope

Born Again

A new day is here
I hear
Myself

I see myself as I was and as I am now
No more falsettos
No more facades
The devil, angel, and referee each play their
parts

I will deliver a sermon that no one will ever
forget
My life will be a testimony of the princess who
was degraded, elevated, ebbed, and flowed her
way to a new beginning

I will write my future on the beaches of Florida
and in the sands of distant shores
My students will be my scribes

5.28.20

For you, it's a passing headline
It's a hashtag
You don't lose sleep
You don't lose friends
You don't lose respect
You don't lose respect for friends

For us its life
Its sanctioned terrorism and we have to hide
behind fake smiles and sympathy for your
discomfort at revealing a truth that no one wants
to hear
The truth that white supremacy thrives because
of white liberals
It is not just a red neck problem
The truth that white fragility is displayed in the
DNA of every American institution
The truth that white lies kill and black lives only
matter for sound bites, for excitement
We are your horror shows turned reality tv in
person
We are your soap operas for when you get off
your soapboxes
And what am I supposed to say

How am I supposed to teach my children that
love is bigger than hate when
You erase every stride
Every pride
Every opportunity to mend the wings that you
tore
Every voice that you have silenced
Every native you raped
Every African you scraped
And meanwhile, all lives matter exists
Meanwhile, blue lives matter wore a shirt saying
I can breathe
Meanwhile, the seeds that are being sown come
with a price
There will be a reckoning
I will not mourn for your loss
You are hardening my heart Amerikkka
And should God save America for a few souls?
Should Allah bestow peace?
Should mother earth allow us to repair that
which has been trampled?
The respect of this planet and the pride of this
globe rests on our shoulders collectively but you
are unwilling to let go of a wrong that you think
we did

Men die building bridges
Women die in childbirth
Fetuses are aborted when they are undesired

Destruction is everywhere and yet the phoenix
rises from the ashes
And yet Sankofa looks over her shoulder and
learns from the past to make a new future
Ashe
Ashe
My life will tell the story of gold
My voice will tell the story of old
My people's spirit was never sold
I will do as Wangari Matthai ordered
I will be a hummingbird!

9 789357 443432